# Mr. Moon and Miss Sun 해님 달님
# The Herdsman and the Weaver 견우와 직녀

Adapted by Duance Vorhees & Mark Mueller
Illustrated by Kim Yon-kyong

HOLLYM

Elizabeth, NJ Seoul

# Mr. Moon and Miss Sun

A long time ago, a widow lived with her son and daughter in a small, remote cottage in the valley.

One day she had to go to a nearby village in order to help prepare a great feast. The children had to stay home alone all day and watch the house. Mother finished her work as soon as she could and headed for home, but the day had already turned dark.

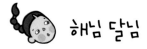 해님 달님 ..................................................................................

옛날 옛날, 산골짜기 조그만 외딴집에 홀어머니와 오누이가 살고 있었습니다.

하루는 어머니가 이웃 마을 잔칫집에 일을 도와 주러 갔습니다.

오누이는 어머니가 빨리 돌아오기를 기다리면서 집을 보고 있었습니다.

어슴푸레 날이 저물어 갔습니다.

어머니는 일을 마치고 서둘러 집으로 향했습니다.

As Mother went over the first hill, she was startled by a huge tiger.

"O-heung!" the tiger roared. Then he walked up to the frightened woman and sniffed.

"If you give me some rice cake," he said, "I won't eat you." Quickly, Mother threw the tiger a rice cake and began running. The tiger swallowed the rice cake in a single gulp and dashed to the next hill. When Mother reached it, the tiger was already on the path in front of her. "If you give me some rice cake, I won't eat you," he said in a strong voice.

The poor woman threw him another rice cake and started to run again. The tiger swallowed the rice cake whole and raced ahead of her. At each hill he waited for her, growling, "If you give me a rice cake, I won't eat you."

어머니가 첫째 고개를 막 넘어서는데, 커다란 호랑이가 '어흥' 하고 나타났습니다.

호랑이는 어머니 옆에 와서 킁킁 냄새를 맡고는 말했습니다.

"그 떡 하나 주면 안 잡아먹지."

어머니는 떡을 던져 주고 또 한 고개를 넘어갔습니다.

그러나 호랑이는, 다음 고개 그 다음 고개에서도 나타나 떡을 달라고 했습니다.

Before long, the woman ~~given~~ *gave* the tiger the last of her rice cakes. So when the tiger said, "If you give me a rice cake, I won't eat you," she had no more to give. So the tiger ate Mother.

It became darker and darker, and Mother still didn't come home. The children became more and more worried.

Little Sister said to her older brother, "Where is mother? I'm scared." Big Brother tried to smile. "Don't worry," he said. "She'll be home very soon. Just wait a little longer."

At that moment, they heard a loud rattling noise as someone tried to open the door latch. Someone outside was saying, "Children, open the door right away, it's your mother."

"Oh! It's Mother!" Little Sister was up in a flash to open the door.

떡을 모두 빼앗아 먹은 호랑이는 어머니마저 날름 잡아먹어 버렸습니다.

깜깜해지도록 어머니가 돌아오지 않자, 오누이는 걱정이 되었습니다.

"오빠, 엄마는 왜 여태 안 오지?" 누이동생이 걱정스레 물었습니다.

"이제 곧 오실 거야, 조금만 더 기다려 보자." 그때 '달각달각' 문고리를 흔드는 소리가 났습니다.

"얘들아, 엄마다. 문 열어라."

"아! 엄마가 왔다." 누이동생은 문을 열어 주려고 깡충 뛰어 일어났습니다.

But Big Brother grabbed her. "Wait!" he said. "That does not sound like Mother's voice." "I caught a cold and my throat is sore," came a harsh voice from outside. "Stop dawdling and open the door right away."

But Big Brother held Little Sister tight. He was not sure what to do. "Show me your hand," he shouted.

A huge, shaggy, yellow paw burst through the paper window.

"잠깐만 기다려. 저건 엄마 목소리가 아니야."

오빠는 누이동생을 붙잡아 앉히고 바깥을 향해 말했습니다.

"우리 엄마 목소리가 아닌걸요."

그러자 바깥에서 대답이 들려왔습니다.

"감기가 들어서 목이 쉬었단다. 어서 꾸물대지 말고 문 열어라."

오빠는 고개를 갸웃거리며 말했습니다.

"그럼 손을 한번 내밀어 봐요."

그러자 창호지를 뚫고 커다란 손이 불쑥 들어왔습니다.

"Oh! That does not look like Mother's hand!" Little Sister cried out. The voice outside said, "I worked very hard today. My hands are very rough. Stop dawdling and open the door right away."

Little Sister squirmed loose from Big Brother and opened the door. "You must be very hungry. I'll fix you something to eat." Then the tiger hurried into the kitchen, who was wearing Mother's clothes.

Big Brother felt sorry. "Poor Mother," he thought. "I'll help fix her meal." But when he looked into the kitchen he saw a tail under Mother's dress. "It's a tiger!" he told himself.

Big Brother thought quickly and calmly led Little Sister outside.

"어머, 이 털 좀 봐! 우리 엄마 손이 아니에요." 누이동생이 소리쳤습니다.

"엄마가 일을 많이 해서 손이 거칠어진 거란다."

오누이는 그제야 머리를 끄덕이며 문을 열어 주었습니다.

"배고팠지, 금방 저녁 지어 줄게." 엄마는 급히 부엌으로 들어갔습니다.

'우리 엄마가 고생이 많으시구나. 가엾은 엄마…….'

이런 생각을 하며 부엌을 들여다보던 오빠는 소스라치게 놀랐습니다.

"앗! 저건 호랑이잖아." 오빠는 허겁지겁 누이동생을 데리고 방을 나왔습니다.

"That is not Mother in the kitchen," he told her. "It's a tiger! We must hide."

Big Brother and Little Sister climbed up the persimmon tree next to the well. Inside, the tiger was warming himself at the kitchen fire. Finally, he licked his chops and said to himself, "The time has come. I'll make a nice little meal out of those two kids." And he flung the door open.

But the house was completely empty. "Where did my meal go?" the tiger wondered.

He ran through the house, turning over the furniture and breaking the dishes as he looked for the two children. Then he happened to see Little Sister's shadow move.

"Ah-ha! They climbed up the tree. That was a silly thing for them to do," the tiger muttered to himself.

"어서 도망가자! 부엌에 있는 건 엄마가 아니라 호랑이야."

오누이는 재빨리 우물 옆에 있는 감나무 위로 올라갔습니다.

"이제 슬슬 녀석들을 잡아먹어 볼까!" 호랑이는 입맛을 쩝쩝 다시며 방문을 열어젖혔습니다.

그런데 방 안은 텅 비어 있었습니다.

"이놈들이 어디로 갔지?" 호랑이는 집 안을 샅샅이 뒤지기 시작했습니다.

그러다가 뒤뜰 마당에 비친 오누이의 그림자를 찾아냈습니다.

'아하! 저놈들이 나무에 올라갔구나. 그렇지만 어림도 없지.'

"Children!" he called up to them. "Why are you climbing tree at night? You might fall. Come down this instant!"

Little Sister began shaking with fright, but she made no move to climb down.

The tiger waited and waited, but the children stayed right where they were. So the tiger tried to climb the tree to catch them.

Every time he got halfway up the trunk he slipped back down.

"How did you climb up there?" the tiger shouted from below.

"It's so slippery that your poor old mother can't climb up. Come down this instant!"

Big Brother thought he would have some fun. "Mother dear, get some sesame oil from the kitchen and rub it all over the trunk," he told the tiger.

"애들아, 이 밤중에 나무엔 뭣하러 올라갔니? 떨어질라, 어서 내려오너라."

오누이는 호랑이에게 들킨 것을 알고 오들오들 떨었습니다.

한참을 기다려도 오누이가 내려오지 않자, 호랑이는 나무에 기어오르기 시작했습니다.

그러나 자꾸만 미끄러졌습니다.

"너희는 어떻게 올라갔니? 엄마는 미끄러워서 올라갈 수가 없구나."

그때 오빠에게 좋은 꾀가 떠올랐습니다. "부엌에서 참기름을 바르고 올라왔지요."

So the tiger did as he was told. He went into the kitchen, found a big jar of sesame oil, and spread it all over the tree trunk. Then he tried to climb the tree again, but of course the sesame oil made it even more slippery. The tiger slid down fast and hard, right on his tail. "Ow!" he cried.

Little Sister could not help laughing. "Silly old fool!" she laughed. "If he used an ax he could climb the tree easily."

Then she realized what she had said and stopped laughing. But it was too late. The tiger had heard what she said. He found an ax and struck the tree. Then he pulled the ax out and struck the tree again, higher. Using the cuts he made as footholds, the tiger was able to make steady progress up the trunk.

호랑이는 얼른 부엌에 있는 참기름을 바르고 나무에 기어올랐습니다.

그러나 호랑이는 자꾸 미끄러지면서 엉덩방아를 찧었습니다.

"하하, 저런 바보! 도끼로 찍고 올라오면 되는데."

누이동생은 웃음을 못 참고 바른대로 가르쳐 주었습니다.

실수를 깨달은 누이동생은 웃음을 멈추었습니다. 그러나 이미 때는 늦었습니다.

호랑이는 도끼를 가져다가 나무를 쿵쿵 찍으며 올라오기 시작했습니다.

Little Sister looked down at the tiger and then up at the sky. "Oh God, please save us," she prayed. "Please send us a rope."

And then as if by magic, a rope dropped gently down from the sky.

Little Sister and Big Brother quickly grabbed the rope and were pulled rapidly into the sky.

Just at that moment, the tiger reached the highest branch. Watching the children disappear into the clouds, he flew into a frenzy. Repeating what he had heard Little Sister say, he prayed, "Oh God, send me a rope too."

A second rope dropped gently down.

"I'm on my way!" the tiger roared and grabbed onto the heavenly rope.

오누이는 하늘을 보며 빌었습니다.

"하느님 저희들을 살려 주세요. 저희들에게 동아줄을 내려 주세요."

그러자 하늘에서 스르르 동아줄 한 가닥이 내려왔습니다.

오누이는 동아줄을 붙잡고 하늘로 둥실 떠올랐습니다.

오누이를 놓쳐서 분통이 터진 호랑이는 오누이를 흉내 내어 빌었습니다.

"하느님 나에게도 동아줄을 내려 주시오."

이번에도 하늘에서 동아줄이 내려왔습니다.

He was pulled high up above the ground. But the rope was rotten. It snapped and he fell and fell, far down to the earth below. When he landed in a millet field, every bone in his body broke.

Big Brother and Little Sister kept going up and up. Big Brother became the sun, shining brightly all day long. And Little Sister became the moon, lighting dark roads at night.

But Little Sister was very frightened to be alone at night, so Big Brother changed places with her.

Even in the daytime, people cannot look at shy Sun's face because she is so bright.

호랑이는 '얼싸, 좋다' 하고 신이 나서 동아줄에 매달렸습니다.

그러나 그것은 썩은 동아줄이었습니다.

호랑이는 줄이 뚝 끊어지는 바람에 수수밭으로 떨어져 죽었습니다.

하늘로 올라간 오누이는 해와 달이 되었습니다.

오빠는 해가 되어 환하게 낮을 비추고 누이동생은 달이 되어 깜깜한 밤길을 밝혀 주었습니다.

그러나 누이동생은 밤에 혼자 다니는 것이 무서워 오빠와 자리를 바꾸었습니다.

우리가 해를 쳐다볼 때 눈이 부신 것은 수줍은 동생이 아무도 자기 얼굴을 못 보게
화살같이 센 빛을 내기 때문이라고 합니다.

# The Herdsman and the Weaver

Once upon a time there lived a great king who watched over the sky. His lovely daughter, the princess, could weave cloth finer and better than anyone.

As a result, the king jokingly referred to her as "his weaver."

The princess's loom would rattle and knock all day long. Her shuttle would move in and out among the threads, changing them into lovely cloth.

 ## 견우와 직녀

까마득한 옛날, 하늘나라를 다스리는 임금님에게 사랑스러운 공주가 있었습니다.

공주는 베를 누구보다 곱게 짜는 솜씨를 가지고 있었습니다.

임금님은 공주의 이름을 직녀라고 지어 주었습니다.

'달각달각…….'

직녀는 언제나 열심히 베를 짰습니다.

그녀의 베 짜는 북은 베틀의 실 사이를 이리저리 오가며 아름다운 옷감을 짜냈습니다.

The princess grew up at her loom and then it was time for her to marry.

The king searched his kingdom high and low for a suitable husband for his daughter. One day he met a young man whom he liked very much. "This young man will make a fine husband for my daughter," the king told himself.

The young man was a herdsman. He had loved cattle ever since he was very young, so he was very happy in his work.

On a beautiful spring day, when all of the flowers were in bloom and the birds were singing, the weaver married herdsman. Everyone in the kingdom was overjoyed to see what a beautiful couple they made.

어느덧 세월이 흘러, 직녀는 시집갈 나이가 되었습니다.

임금님은 직녀의 신랑감을 찾아 나라 안을 두루 돌아다녔습니다.

그러던 어느 날, 임금님은 마음에 꼭 드는 신랑감을 만났습니다.

바로 견우라는 청년이었습니다.

견우는 소를 좋아해서 어릴 때부터 늘 소를 몰고 다녔습니다.

꽃들이 활짝 핀 봄날, 견우와 직녀는 결혼식을 올렸습니다.

온 나라 사람들이 견우와 직녀의 결혼을 함께 기뻐했습니다.

After the wedding, the newlyweds spent everyday roaming in the fields together. The herdsman no longer paid attention to the cows. So the cows wandered into the royal garden and trampled the royal flowerbed, ruining it.

The weaver no longer wove cloth. A thick layer of gray dust gathered on her loom.

When the king saw what was happening, he became very worried. Calling them to him, he told the herdsman, "Son, you are still a herdsman. You must watch your cows better!" He looked at his daughter and said to her, "You must not abandon your loom!"

결혼을 한 견우와 직녀는 매일 들판을 쏘다니며 즐겁게 놀았습니다.

견우는 소를 돌보지 않았습니다.

견우의 소는 대궐의 꽃밭을 마구 밟아서 망가뜨렸습니다.

직녀는 베를 짜지 않았습니다.

직녀의 베틀에는 뽀얗게 먼지가 쌓였습니다.

이것을 본 임금님은 걱정이 되어 두 사람을 불렀습니다.

"견우는 소를 잘 돌봐 주고, 직녀는 열심히 베를 짜도록 하여라."

But the herdsman and the weaver, who were still just children even though they were married, paid no attention to the king. They kept roaming in the fields and playing games.

The king became very angry. He scolded them loudly. "How do you expect to live if you don't work? Since you will not obey me I must punish you. From now on, the herdsman must live in the Eastern sky. The weaver must live in the Western sky."

When the herdsman and the weaver heard this, they both cried, "Oh, Father, please forgive us. We know we were wrong but we'll change. Please let us stay together. We love each other so much!"

But the king was not moved by their tears.

견우와 직녀는 노는 데 빠져 임금님의 말을 듣지 않았습니다.

임금님은 크게 화가 나서 견우와 직녀를 꾸짖었습니다.

"너희들은 어찌하여 일을 하지 않고 살아가려고 하느냐. 그 잘못에 대한 벌을 내리겠노라. 이제부터 견우는 동쪽 나라로 직녀는 서쪽 나라로 헤어져 살도록 하여라."

"아버님 저희가 잘못했습니다. 제발 저희들을 함께 살 수 있도록 해 주십시오."

견우와 직녀는 임금님께 용서를 빌었습니다.

그러나 임금님의 화는 풀리지 않았습니다.

The herdsman and the weaver were forced to part. He went East and she went West.

They were so sad that the king felt sorry for them. He decided to let them meet just once a year on the banks of the Milky Way river.

All year long, the two lovers counted the days and thought about each other. They deeply regretted their earlier thoughtlessness.

견우와 직녀는 울면서 동쪽 나라와 서쪽 나라로 길을 떠났습니다.

임금님은 두 사람이 가엾게 느껴졌습니다.

그래서 임금님은 일 년에 한 번씩 은하수 강가에서 두 사람이 만나는 것을 허락했습니다.

견우와 직녀는 서로 만날 날만 손꼽아 기다리며 살았습니다.

그리고 지난 날의 잘못을 깊이 뉘우쳤습니다.

The day finally came for them to meet. With high hopes, each headed for the Milky Way river. But when they reached it, it was so wide and the night so dark that they could not see each other.

드디어 견우와 직녀가 만나는 날이 되었습니다.

두 사람은 부푼 가슴을 안고 은하수를 향하여 길을 떠났습니다.

견우와 직녀는 한달음에 은하수 강가에 닿았습니다.

그러나 강가에 선 두 사람은 눈앞이 캄캄했습니다.

은하수는 말할 수 없이 넓고 큰 강이었기 때문입니다.

The herdsman and the weaver stood on the banks of the Milky Way and cried. Their tears rolled down their cheeks and into the river. They flowed down the river and became rain. The rain that had been their tears fell to the earth, until the ground was completely covered with water. The seas rose and rose.

The fields and gardens were flooded, and the homes of the people were swept away.

견우와 직녀는 은하수 강가에서 슬프게 울었습니다.

두 사람의 눈물은 쉴 새 없이 흘러 내려 은하수에 떨어졌습니다.

은하수에 떨어진 눈물은 비가 되어 땅에 내렸습니다.

그러자 땅 위는 온통 물바다가 되었습니다.

논과 밭이 물에 잠기고 집들이 무너졌습니다.

The animals became very alarmed. They all met to decide what to do. Each animal spoke in turn. Some had low grunts and some had high squeaks. Some of them whistled when they talked. One animal insisted, "We must help the herdsman and the weaver get together, or this rain will never stop."

"Yes," said another, "we must build a bridge or something."

"That's it!" exclaimed another animal. "We must build a great bridge!" All of the animals agreed. But none of them really knew how to go about building a bridge. They all stood around looking from one to another, twisting their tails in silence.

Finally, some crows and magpies spoke up. "Let us birds do it," said one. "We can fly to the Milky Way river," said another, "And make ourselves into a bridge."

땅 위의 짐승들은 걱정이 되어 회의를 열었습니다.

짐승들은 웅성거리며 저마다 한마디씩 했습니다.

"이 비를 그치게 하려면 견우와 직녀가 만나도록 해줘야 합니다."

"그러면 다리를 놓아야 할 텐데……."

짐승들은 이렇게 입을 모았지만, 좋은 수가 떠오르지 않았습니다.

그때 까마귀와 까치가 나와서 말했습니다.

"우리는 높이 날 수가 있어요. 우리가 은하수에 올라가 다리를 놓겠어요."

So all of the crows in the world, and their cousins the magpies, flew up to the Milky Way river. They flew tightly together and held on to each other with their talons and soon they stretched from bank to bank.

The herdsman and the weaver were very surprised to see a bridge of birds. "What's this?" they exclaimed. "We can cross the Milky Way river now!"

Each one started running across the backs of the birds. In the middle of the bridge they met and happily hugged each other.

드디어 은하수에 다리를 놓는 일이 시작되었습니다.

온 세상에 있는 까치와 까마귀는 모두 은하수로 올라갔습니다.

'때깍때깍, 까악까악······.'

수많은 까치와 까마귀들이 줄을 지어 길고 튼튼한 다리를 만들었습니다.

"아니, 이게 웬 다리일까?"

견우와 직녀는 어리둥절하여 눈물을 멈추었습니다.

"이제는 은하수를 건널 수 있게 되었어!"

그리고는 단숨에 다리를 건너, 서로 부둥켜안고 기뻐했습니다.

The heavy rains slowed to a drizzle. But then the two lovers had to return to their homes in the East and West for another lonely year.

Every year after that, on the seventh day of the seventh moon, all of the crows and magpies would fly to the Milky Way river to form a bridge. The herdsman and the weaver would meet on that day by crossing the river on the backs of the birds.

And that is why the crows and magpies always lose their feathers after the seventh day of the seventh moon. The old feathers become damaged when the herdsman and the weaver walk across the crow-and-magpie bridge.

땅 위에 심하게 내리던 비는 뚝 그쳤습니다.

그러나 이 두 사람은 또다시 외로운 일 년을 보내기 위해 동쪽과 서쪽의 집으로 돌아가야 했습니다.

해마다 칠월 칠석이 되면 까마귀와 까치는 은하수에 올라가 다리를 놓았습니다.

견우와 직녀는 그 다리에서 일 년에 한 번씩 만날 수 있게 되었습니다.

사람들은 까마귀와 까치가 놓은 다리를 '오작교'라고 불렀습니다.

그리고 칠월 칠석이 지난 뒤에 까마귀와 까치의 머리털이 벗겨지는 까닭은 이 날 견우와 직녀을 위한 다리가 되어서 밟혔기 때문이라고 믿었습니다.

## 해님 달님 / 견우와 직녀

1990년 3월 5일 1판 1쇄 발행
2007년 5월 15일 2판 1쇄 발행

엮은이 D. Vorhees & M. Mueller
그린이 김연경

펴낸이 임상백
펴낸곳 (주)한림출판사
주소 (110-111) 서울특별시 종로구 관철동 13-13 종로코아
등록 1963년 1월 18일 제 300-1963-1호
전화 02-735-7551~4 ∣ 전송 02-730-8192, 5149
전자우편 info@hollym.co.kr ∣ 홈페이지 www.hollym.co.kr

미국 동시 발행 Hollym International Corp.
18 Donald Place, Elizabeth, NJ 07208
Tel: (908) 353-1655  Fax: (908) 353-0255
http://www. hollym.com

인쇄 삼성인쇄(주) ∣ 제책 신안제책

ISBN-10: 0-930878-72-8
ISBN-13: 978-0-930878-72-6

* 값은 뒤표지에 있습니다.
* 잘못 만든 책은 구입하신 곳에서 바꾸어 드립니다.